POCKET POSITIVITY
RUPAUL

POCKET POSITIVITY
RUPAUL

**The life-affirming philosophy
of a drag superstar**

Hardie Grant

BOOKS

CONTENTS

LOVE YOURSELF
7

EAT THE WORLD
25

CHOOSE JOY
43

LIVE YOUR TRUTH
63

HAVE A PARTY
83

LOVE YOURSELF

'NEVER SAVE BATH BOMBS FOR LATER. NEVER WAIT FOR A SPECIAL OCCASION TO LIGHT CANDLES. DON'T WAIT TO BOOK A MASSAGE . . .

. . . TREAT YOURSELF TO
A SPA DAY. GET YOURSELF
A COLONIC IMMEDIATELY.
NOW IS THE TIME.'

'LOOKING GOOD IS
A CELEBRATION OF YOURSELF,
IT'S LIKE SAYING TO YOUR
CREATOR, "I LOVE IT, I'M
GONNA DECORATE IT."'

'WALKING WITH YOUR CHEST OUT AND YOUR HEAD HELD HIGH SAYS YOU HAVE EARNED THE RIGHT TO STOMP AND PUMMEL THIS PARTICULAR PIECE OF REAL ESTATE.'

'IF YOU CAN'T LOVE YOURSELF, HOW IN THE HELL YOU GONNA LOVE SOMEBODY ELSE?'

'LIFE CAN BE DAUNTING, BUT NOT IMPOSSIBLE, IF APPROACHED FROM A FOUNDATION OF SELF-LOVE.'

'EVERYBODY SAY LOVE!'

'WILLINGLY RELEASE THE HURT. DON'T LET THE HEARTACHE DEFINE YOU.'

'YOU HAVE EVERY RIGHT
TO BECOME BITTER.
YOUR MIND WILL
TELL YOU, "F THIS.
F ALL OF THIS." . . .

... DON'T TAKE THE BAIT. CONTINUE TO LOVE YOURSELF. THAT'S WHERE YOUR POWER IS RIGHT THERE.'

'KNOWING WHAT YOU WANT TO DO IN LIFE IS USUALLY NOT DIFFICULT . . .

'... WHAT IS DIFFICULT IS CARVING OUT THE TIME IT TAKES TO INVEST IN YOU.'

'ONCE YOUR FREQUENCY IS OPEN, THEN THE LOVE WILL FLOW THROUGH YOU.'

'I'VE ALWAYS SAID THAT IT'S BEST TO LOOK YOUR BEST WHEN YOU FEEL YOUR WORST. YOU'VE GOT TO FAKE IT UNTIL YOU MAKE IT.'

'YOU HAVE THE POWER TO MOVE ON IF YOU'RE WILLING TO LET GO OF THE LIMITED PERCEPTION YOU HAVE OF YOURSELF.'

'FOCUS ON YOUR BREATHING!
IT WILL REALLY HELP YOU WITH
YOUR CONFIDENCE BECAUSE
IT WILL REMIND YOU WHO
YOU REALLY ARE.'

EAT THE
WORLD

'FULFILMENT ISN'T FOUND OVER THE RAINBOW – IT'S FOUND IN THE HERE AND NOW.'

'YOU GO OUT THERE AND YOU KNOCK THEM DEAD, BECAUSE YOU ARE A WINNER, BABY!'

'I LOVE TO LAUGH, I LOVE COLOUR, I LOVE TEXTURE AND I LOVE CREATIVITY.'

'USE ALL THE COLOURS, TOUCH ALL THE TOYS AND LICK ALL THE CANDY! DO IT ALL.'

'YOU HAVE TO GO OUT THERE AND OWN WHAT IT MEANS TO BE A BADASS BITCH.'

'NOW GO FORTH, AND BE SICKENING.'

'THE EGO SAYS: IF YOU GET A PIECE OF THE PIZZA THAT MEANS THERE'S LESS FOR ME . . .

... THE TRUTH IS THE WHOLE WORLD IS FULL OF PIZZA, ENOUGH FOR EVERYONE.'

'DON'T LET PEOPLE OR SOCIETY OR YOUR IDEA OF YOURSELF KEEP YOU FROM LIVING THIS LIFE AND ENJOYING ALL THIS LIFE HAS TO OFFER.'

'USE ALL THE COLOURS IN THE CRAYON BOX.'

'IF AT FIRST YOU DON'T SUCCEED, BECOME A LEGEND, HUNTY!'

'LIVE YOUR LIFE IN THE NOW, BECAUSE YOU GET TO A CERTAIN AGE AND YOU REALISE, "WOW, THAT WAS FAST."'

'RISE UP AND BE FEARLESS, LIKE A MAASAI WARRIOR. STAKE YOUR CLAIM IN THIS LIFETIME.'

'LIFE'S JOURNEY – IT UNFOLDS FOR YOU AS YOU ARE READY FOR IT.'

'INSIDE OF US ALL IS GREAT POWER, CREATIVITY AND BEAUTY.'

'FIND THE LIFE YOU WANT. FIND ALL THAT LIFE HAS TO OFFER.'

CHOOSE JOY

'IT'S VERY EASY TO LOOK AT THE WORLD AND THINK, THIS IS ALL SO CRUEL AND SO MEAN . . .

. . . IT'S IMPORTANT TO NOT BECOME BITTER FROM IT. '

'HAPPINESS IS WANTING WHAT YOU ALREADY HAVE.'

'CONTRARY TO POPULAR BELIEF, A GORGEOUS HEART AND SOUL WILL TAKE YOU FURTHER THAN GOOD LOOKS.'

'TODAY I DEFINE SUCCESS
BY THE FLUIDITY WITH WHICH
I TRANSCEND EMOTIONAL
LANDMINES AND CHOOSE JOY
AND GRATITUDE INSTEAD.'

'CLEAR OUT THE BLOCKAGE THAT KEEPS YOU PLAYING SMALL, KEEPS YOU LISTENING TO THE NEGATIVE STORIES IN YOUR HEAD, KEEPS YOU IN THE DARKNESS AND MOVE FORWARD INTO THE LIGHT.'

'I THINK THAT SWEETNESS AND KINDNESS ARE AT THE TOP OF MY LIST OF HUMAN VIRTUES.'

'IN A CULTURE,
YOU CAN CHOOSE
FEAR OR LOVE.'

'IF YOU'RE GORGEOUS-LOOKING ACCORDING TO *VOGUE* MAGAZINE AND YOU HAVE AN EVIL HEART . . .

. . . THAT MAKES YOU REALLY UGLY IN MY BOOK.'

'NEVER FORGET THAT THE MOST POLITICAL THING YOU CAN EVER DO IS FOLLOW YOUR HEART.'

'THE GIFT YOU CAN GIVE
TO OTHER PEOPLE IS
ALLOWING THEM TO GIVE
YOU SOMETHING.'

'IF YOU'RE IN A SITUATION WHEN YOU ARE WITH SOMEONE WHO YOU DON'T HAVE ANYTHING IN COMMON WITH, FIND SOMETHING THAT YOU LOVE ABOUT THEM . . .

. . . BECAUSE IN THE END IT'S ACTUALLY FOR YOU, YOU FORGIVE PEOPLE NOT FOR THEM BUT FOR YOU.'

'IT TAKES A LOT OF HARD WORK TO REMAIN POSITIVE . . .

...BUT POSITIVITY ALWAYS PAYS OFF.'

'THE ONLY WAY YOU'RE GOING TO GET THROUGH THIS THING IS TO LAUGH.'

'THE KEY IS TO REMEMBER TO KEEP YOURSELF UP AND KEEP ON WALKING.'

LIVE YOUR TRUTH

'WHAT IT SAYS ON
YOUR DRIVER'S LICENSE
ISN'T REALLY WHO YOU ARE
– YOU ARE SOMETHING MUCH
GREATER THAN THAT.'

'OUR CULTURE IS ADDICTED
TO FEAR AND THE FLAT
SCREEN IS OUR DRUG DEALER.
DON'T ALLOW THAT CRAP
INTO YOUR HEAD!'

'YOU ARE NONE OF THE SUPERFICIAL THINGS THAT THIS WORLD DEEMS IMPORTANT . . .

. . . THE REAL YOU IS THE ENERGY FORCE THAT CREATED THE ENTIRE UNIVERSE!'

'KNOW THYSELF, KNOW YOUR HISTORY AND KNOW HOW TO READ THE LANDSCAPE.'

'WHEN THE GOING GETS TOUGH, THE TOUGH REINVENT.'

'DON'T BE SORRY. BE FIERCE.'

'YOU JUST DO YOU, YOU KNOW?'

'REMEMBER WHO
YOU REALLY ARE. UNLEASH
THE DRAGON AND LET – THESE
– BITCHES – HAVE – IT!'

'IF YOU PAY ATTENTION TO YOUR HEART AND NOT WHAT OTHER PEOPLE SAY, YOU PROBABLY WILL HAVE A REALLY GOOD TIME HERE ON THIS PLANET.'

'KNOW YOUR RHYTHM, KNOW WHAT IT IS THAT MAKES YOU, YOU.'

'STOP TRYING TO FIT IN WHEN YOU WERE BORN TO STAND OUT.'

'SUCCESS IS SOMETHING BETWEEN YOU AND YOURSELF. I THINK ONLY YOU KNOW WHERE YOU'VE COME FROM AND HOW FAR YOU WANNA GO.'

'WHEN YOU BECOME THE IMAGE OF YOUR OWN IMAGINATION, IT'S THE MOST POWERFUL THING YOU COULD EVER DO.'

'ONCE YOU GET RID OF
. . . EVERYTHING AND
EVERYONE THAT MIGHT
BE BLOCKING YOU,
YOU WILL LIVE IN
THE LIGHT.'

'KNOW WHO YOU ARE AND DELIVER IT AT ALL TIMES.'

'THE SECRET OF SUCCESS IN EVERY FIELD IS REDEFINING WHAT SUCCESS MEANS TO YOU. IT CAN'T BE YOUR PARENT'S DEFINITION, THE MEDIA'S DEFINITION . . .

... OR YOUR NEIGHBOUR'S DEFINITION. OTHERWISE, SUCCESS WILL NEVER SATISFY YOU.'

'THAT IS THE KEY TO NAVIGATING THIS LIFE – DON'T TAKE IT TOO SERIOUSLY. THAT'S WHEN THE PARTY BEGINS.'

'MAKE LOVE. LOVE PEOPLE. BE SWEET. HAVE CORN DOGS. DANCE. LIVE. LOVE. FUCK SHIT UP.'

'ENJOY IT NOW, BUY YOU A SYNTHETIC WIG, GET YOU A PAIR OF CHA-CHA HEELS, GET YOUR DRIVER'S LICENSE, AND HIT THE ROAD, BABY.'

'ONCE YOU GET OFF THAT STAGE,
SEE YOURSELF AS A CONSTRUCT,
THEN YOU CAN HAVE A PARTY –
THAT'S WHEN YOU CAN
HAVE SOME FUN.'

'MY MISSION STATEMENT IS: I CAME TO THIS PLANET TO HAVE A GREAT TIME, HAVE FUN, MEET PEOPLE, DO FUN THINGS.'

'NEVER PASS UP
AN OPPORTUNITY
TO WEAR A FANCY
OUTFIT, EVEN IF YOU'RE
THE ONLY ONE WHO
APPRECIATES IT.'

'LIVE YOUR LIFE WITH NO RESTRICTIONS.'

'DON'T. TAKE. LIFE. TOO. FUCKING. SERIOUSLY.'

'YOU HAVE TO BE BEAUTY *AND* THE BEAST, YOU HAVE TO BE BERRY GORDY *AND* DIANA ROSS . . .

. . . YOU HAVE TO BE SONNY *AND* CHER, DO YOU FOLLOW? LET THE CHURCH SAY AMEN.'

Sources

'Interview: RuPaul , America's first drag superstar', 2011, PinkNews, pinknews.co.uk – pp. 32–33

'It Got Better featuring RuPaul | L/Studio Created by Lexus', 2015, LStudio, youtube.com – pp. 16– 17; p. 74

'Q&A: RuPaul on eyelash curlers, shapewear, his TV show and new book', 2010, Los Angeles Times, latimesblogs.latimes.com – pp. 80–81

Alnuweiri, T, 2017, '5 Times RuPaul Was Your Unofficial Life Coach', Well + Good, wellandgood.com – pp. 58–59; p. 76; p. 79

Commons, J, 2015, 'RuPaul Gives Us The Best Life Advice Ever', Grazia, graziadaily.co.uk – pp. 18–19; p. 20; p. 21; p. 23; pp. 56–57

Fagan, G and Ella Walker, 2016, 'RuPaul: Taking Drag mainstream', The Press and Journal, pressandjournal.co.uk – p. 73

Frank, A, 2015, 'Drag Race Is Back! RuPaul on What Makes a Queen a Star', Vogue, vogue.com – p. 68

Jung, E. A, 2016, 'Real Talk With RuPaul', Vulture, vulture.com – p. 85

Megarry, D, 2017, '5 inspirational RuPaul quotes to help you live your best life', Gay Times, gaytimes.co.uk – p. 10

Munzenrieder, K, 2017, 'The Gospel According to RuPaul: 10 Inspiring Quotes Before the Return of RuPaul's Drag Race', W Magazine, wmagazine.com – p. 26; pp. 44–45; p. 48; p. 64; p. 77; p. 84

Nichols, J. M, 2017, 'RuPaul on Trump: "Pardon Me Madame, But The Emperor Has No Clothes!"', Huffpost, huffpost.com – p. 39; p. 54

Nicholson, R, 2015, 'RuPaul: "Drag is dangerous. We are making fun of everything"', The Guardian, theguardian.com – p. 30

Parks-Ramage, J, 2016, 'Sipping and Spilling Tea with RuPaul', VICE, vice.com – p. 29; p. 88

Pocket RuPaul Wisdom, 2017, Hardie Grant Books – p. 27; p. 34; p. 47; p. 51; pp. 52–53; p. 86; p. 87; pp. 92–93

RuPaul, 2018, GuRu, HarperCollins – pp. 8–9; p. 15; p. 22; p. 35; p. 37; p. 40; p. 41; p. 46; p. 49; p. 55; p. 61; p. 75; p. 78; p. 89

RuPaul, 2010, Workin' It! RuPaul's Guide to Life, Liberty and the Pursuit of Style, HarperCollins – p. 11; p. 13; p. 38; p. 65; pp. 66–67; p. 69; p. 72; p. 90

RuPaul's Drag Race, Seasons 1–11, VH1 –
p. 12; p. 14; p. 31; p. 36; p. 70; p. 71

Sunnucks, J, 2016, 'Dolly Parton x RuPaul',
DAZED, dazeddigital.com – p. 50; p. 60

Wu, J, 2013, 'The Transformer: RuPaul',
Interview, interviewmagazine.com – p. 28

Zamora, C and Chris Lam, 2016, 'RuPaul
Gave Us the Best Pieces of Advice for
All Aspiring Drag Queens', Buzzfeed,
buzzfeed.com – p. 91

Pocket Positivity: RuPaul

Published in 2019 by Hardie Grant Books,
an imprint of Hardie Grant Publishing

Hardie Grant Books (London)
5th & 6th Floors
52–54 Southwark Street
London, SE1 1UN

Hardie Grant Books (Melbourne)
Building 1, 658 Church Street
Richmond, Victoria 3121

hardiegrantbooks.com

British Library Cataloguing-in-Publication Data. A catalogue record for this
book is available from the British Library.

ISBN: 978-1-78488-318-8

10 9 8 7 6 5 4 3 2 1

Publishing Director: Kate Pollard
Junior Editor: Bex Fitzsimons
Designer: Studio Noel
Illustrator: Michele Rosenthal

Colour Reproduction by p2d
Printed and bound in China by Leo Paper Products Ltd.